If The Sky Won't Have Me

Poems

By

Anne Leigh Parrish

If The Sky Won't Have Me
Copyright © 2023 Anne Leigh Parrish
Artwork Copyright © Lydia Selk
All Rights Reserved
Published by Unsolicited Press
Printed in the United States of America
First Edition

No part of this book may be used or reproduced in any manner whatsoever without written permission except in the case of brief quotations embodied in critical articles or reviews.

Attention schools, libraries, and businesses: this title can be ordered through Ingram. For special sales, email sales@unsolicitedpress.com.

For information contact:
Unsolicited Press
Portland, Oregon
www.unsolicitedpress.com
orders@unsolicitedpress.com
619-354-8005

Cover Design: Kathryn Gerhardt
Artwork: Lydia Selk
Editor: S.R. Stewart
ISBN: 978-1-956692-52-5

To John, Bob, Lauren, Lacey & Sam

Acknowledgments

"Blue Obsidian"	*Full House Literary Magazine*
"If The Sky Won't Have Me"	*FEED*
"In Her Blindness"	*talking about strawberries all of the time*
"Like A Shade Of Dawn"	*Libretto Magazine*
"No Matter"	*talking about strawberries all of the time*
"Not Seeing Eye To Eye"	*Feminine Collective*
"Our Myths"	*talking about strawberries all of the time*
"Owner's Manual"	*Squawk Back*
"Pothole"	*The Nonconformist Magazine*
"Rage"	*Sledgehammer Lit*
"Resistance"	*Feminine Collective*
"Shift"	*talking about strawberries all of the time*
"Snow Country"	*Humana Obscura*

"That Promising Day"	*talking about strawberries all of the time*
"Truth & Lie"	*Feminine Collective*

Poems

Snow Country	13
The Dance	15
In Turn	16
A Different Hunger	17
Above Us	19
Where The Water Flows	21
Keep Breathing	23
Resistance	25
Below The Surface	27
Truth & Lie	30
Square By Square	32
As One	34
Like A Shade Of Dawn	38
Motel Rooms	40
To Have & To Hold	43
Neither	46
Transit	48
Twinkling	49
Still Out There	52
No Matter	54
Maybe Love	56

Wreckage	59
Gone	61
Challenge	64
Resolutions	66
That Promising Day	68
I Witness My Mother's Death	70
A Lovely Family	72
Crossing	74
Walk On	77
Her Face Curls	79
Guilt	81
Dollhouse	83
This Child Of Theirs	85
These Days	87
Green Sun	89
Trick The Prying Eye	90
More Softly	92
Rage	94
Wake The Hell Up	96
Muon	98
It Never Did	100
A Temple	102
Pothole	103

Not Seeing Eye To Eye	105
Lecture One Of Two	107
Lecture Two Of Two	108
Threshold	109
Our Myths	110
A Gratified Eye	111
The Seed	113
Florist	114
For Georgia	116
On Display	119
Return	121
Almost Perfect	123
Not All Secrets	124
Backstory	127
Ask The Sea	130
Gorgeous Days	133
Come Home	135
Lie Down	136
From Joy	137
See How We Belong	139
Little Cautions	141
Owner's Manual	142
Paths Not Taken	144
Three Gifts	145

Blue Obsidian	147
Flatirons	149
Shift	150
An Impression	151
Brilliant Country	153
August	154
Put Me Out	155
In Her Blindness	157
If The Sky Won't Have Me	159

If The Sky Won't Have Me

If The Sky Won't Have Me

Snow Country

Inside a house with blue walls
One shuts out the world
To make a palace for the heart

Ice clads dust & floats to earth
Eases a hard line, softens an edge

In certain light, drifts are tinged
With blue

The color of the season isn't white or
Gray

Just this gentle hue
Carried within us like
A piece of sky
Waiting for spring

Anne Leigh Parrish

The Dance

Blow-down drapes the lane,
Little branches snapped off,
The wind had a lot to say,
Clumps of moss & cedar leaves
Settle for the car to flatten, the dog to sniff,
The dedicated daily walker to step over

The wind moves on,
There & then not there,
Those pressure changes, high to low,
Give the forest its
Rush & sudden stillness

This is the dance we watch from the safety
Of our study shelter,
Spurred by our own restlessness,
That aching need
To join in

Anne Leigh Parrish

In Turn

Branch moss tinges blue
Berries redden
Fern fronds root in the
Trunk of a big-leaf maple

The dead are all around us in these buds
& blossoms
Puddle's rippling surface
Tree frog's rich call

Standing here, stunned as we
Always are by the indifference of
Nature to anything we want
We remember them & hope to
Be remembered in turn

If The Sky Won't Have Me

A Different Hunger

The robins peg about on the lawn
Skewering worms the water-logged soil
Evicts
They're fat, bossy birds
Who give the dark-eyed juncos hell
Chasing them off,
Dive-bombing them, even

Rising to a branch
Deep in the neighbor's fir
A stellar's jay flashes his gorgeous
Blue
A shade so rich & rare
We don't know its name

The robins don't care about the jay
As long as he holds his perch
I, too, will him to
Remain & fill my empty eye

Anne Leigh Parrish

Until he is called by a different hunger
To share his beauty elsewhere

Above Us

I call anything above me sky
He says God is above us
& I say sure, but you can't see that
& he says, oh no, I see God
Everywhere, every day, even when I
Look at you

It's better to focus on the sky &
Know it's sky
Leave mysticism out of it
Leave the pious men to
Their burning stakes

Just look up & see clouds
Doing what clouds do
Drift, scud, gather
Motion & movement
Blue to gray
Changing the light
& wind

Anne Leigh Parrish

Isn't that enough to feel
In the presence of what's holy?

If The Sky Won't Have Me

Where The Water Flows

When the world burns
Go where the water flows

Escape cinders & black earth
Just go where the water flows

Maps are marked by a river's run
As it carves its way to the sea

Choose any bank
Sit
Hear the rush
Forget drought & dust
Red suns
Fields of ash

Dream instead of gray skies & rain—

Go where the water flows

If The Sky Won't Have Me

Keep Breathing

Mount Rainier grays under the heat dome
Colorado River dries
Phoenicians will surely thirst

The governor of Florida advocates for a virus
While swearing a woman cannot rid her body
Of something the size of a blueberry

Reason burns away like trees out west
Equity is lost

But—

New voices speak in new terms
His husband, her wife
Offer new mandates
Share your identifiers

As land is swallowed by rising seas
& the patriarchy holds fast

Anne Leigh Parrish

We loosen their grip just enough
To keep breathing

If The Sky Won't Have Me

Resistance

Monkey sees men through glass, so glad not to belong
Spider hangs in her summer web, already feels the fall

Upstream fish prefers to drift when choosing not to spawn
Crow departs the evergreen branch, ignores the murder
Behind

Fox in silence takes her prey, will not be called a thief
Hungry doe nibbles the hedge, no care for the gardener's hand

Woman demands he meet her eye & look into her soul
Citizen votes though the process is flawed, will not become
Their fool

Light turns dark as the heavens wheel by, returns when night
Is done
Walk by the fence as it rises & falls, slip through the gap
Toward home

Persuade one person to respect your rights, stand firm against
The rest

Anne Leigh Parrish

Court those who float along the edge, hold the center when
You can

If The Sky Won't Have Me

Below The Surface

The bird slides below the surface of the water &
You say you don't know me

You want to eat me as the bird scarfs
The salt-water morsel

I'm a part of you that has no name
Since mine isn't good enough

Or right
Or logical

Who the hell is applying logic here?

You

Always searching for what fits

The bird rises from the water &
Floats

Anne Leigh Parrish

She is nameless, too,
Known by her markings &
Habits, the waterways she frequents
& those trying to assess her value

She won't be eaten, though

I'm grateful one of us has been
Spared that fate

If The Sky Won't Have Me

Truth & Lie

Moss clings to branches like whispers feather
Hope
Thirty, forty feet up?

Far enough to cramp the neck

Yellow-green & tinged with blue
Delicious to the eye

Airy & light in the warming breeze
Teasing about the season just now
Gone

Moss scratches
Never glides along the skin
Nothing soft or silly about it
As its frail wispiness might suggest

If The Sky Won't Have Me

Sturdy, rugged stuff
Evolved, went one way, then another,
Which improved its chances

Nice to be reminded things
Aren't always as they seem, even if
Truth at first disappoints

Anne Leigh Parrish

Square By Square

Each of us is a patchwork quilt
Made of opposing patterns & pieces
Brooders joke
Gigglers weep
Weepers leave off weeping & laugh with joy

All these contradictions say we're not one thing all the time
      Even the sky's blue differs
Square by square

What use, to recall our complexity?

Don't we already know none of us is a flat plane?

It's clumping people together that gives the false view
All women, *all* men, *all* people of color, *all* people of
This, *all* people of that

There is no all

If The Sky Won't Have Me

Only for the cruel & lazy
Pigeonholers wanting to justify their abuse

The quilt won't be folded away because it's not one hue
Or held together with one kind of stitch

Hang it on the wall if the bed feels wrong
      Or ditch the simile & look me in the eye

Like you, I'm full of surprises

Anne Leigh Parrish

As One

Aunt Ivy gave advice like a cloud gives rain
Never when you want it

What made her pour was a sad face
But not right off

First, there were cookies or a slice of cake
Woe to the calorie counter if Aunt Ivy found you blue

After sweets came questions
Deep, probing, & personal

The tongue-tied struggled to answer
Those naturally discreet shrugged

Aunt Ivy read them as a Gypsy might
Read tea leaves

Be kin to the wider world, she said,
& offered us her path

If The Sky Won't Have Me

Once, in a bad way, bereft & alone
She sat by a stone in England
Erected by men & women who
Worshipped the
Wheeling sky

Be like that stone, she said
Weather, wear away slowly
Shed rain, take up sun's heat
Even let children climb on you
Before their parents
Pull them back

& if that fails,
Consider the people who
Put you there
Their passion to celebrate mystery
See them linking
Hands all around you
Breathing together
Circling one way
Then back

Anne Leigh Parrish

Always in joy
Always as one

If The Sky Won't Have Me

Anne Leigh Parrish

Like A Shade Of Dawn

In shadow the glow is soft
In sunlight, it's hard candy
A room in a house through
Trees with a purple-pink light

You can't read by it
Draw by it
Knit a sweater or
Darn a sock

You can lie, though,
Surrounded by how it
Makes you feel

Which is . . . ?

Poised
Ready to embark
With the color inside
Draped on a rib

If The Sky Won't Have Me

Rising & falling
With the breath

This is a shade for
Adventure
Discovery
Movement
Slow glides & small
Stops

This is the color of someone
Ready to leave it all behind

Anne Leigh Parrish

Motel Rooms

When I was green, crazy,
In love with mountain light
I cleaned motel rooms
Changed sheets & scrubbed toilets
Rubber gloves felt like a gift from God—

As to the guests, just ordinary people
A few crazy fucks
The guy just out of
Prison in Montana told me
He was seeking God
I wanted to offer him my
Gloves
He wasn't the kind to
Scrub anything—

Some rooms were like little apartments
Kitchen, couch,
A table & chairs by the window
Which looked onto the parking lot

If The Sky Won't Have Me

A pregnant woman sat in hers
While her husband was at work
Waiting hour after hour for him to return—

She loved baby powder
It was everywhere, every day
When I came in
Maybe it gave her ovarian cancer
Years later, they say it can do that
Some people were tidy, some
Puked in the bed, missed the toilet
Smeared the mirror
With things I didn't look at too closely—

One man rented a room, one of the owner's best
She said with pride, which meant it had
New curtains & a new bathmat,
& this man went in, wet
A washcloth, lay down, then left a little while later—

Just needed those few moments to
Reckon whatever was behind him
Or maybe to sober up

Anne Leigh Parrish

Call home, say he was on the way
Or never coming back

If The Sky Won't Have Me

To Have & To Hold

Get what you pay for girl, she said
& offered me a box for
All that gorgeous uneaten pasta

Never does to leave any behind
You might want it again later

I knew a man who kept everything
Even his wife's old breast pump
Thinking when the end came he could
Sell it to a desperate, lactating woman

Also on the basement shelf were
Rows of his kids' shoes, long outgrown
Containers of expired vitamins
A broken toaster
Empty plastic picture frames
A cat's collar

Anne Leigh Parrish

All these things had great value to him
Not for what they'd been, but for what
They could one day become

Faith in resurrection, perhaps
Or reincarnation
Or just wanting a second chance

To have & to hold
Keep & clutch
Leave nothing behind

But where that pasta was concerned,
The server was right—
I got peckish before bed
& was grateful for her advice

If The Sky Won't Have Me

Neither

You're my god, but what whimsy you have
Temperamental & reluctant
Inconsistent, too
There, but not really
Sure as hell not when I need you

But you might know me so well

[Of course better than I can ever
Know myself—
This is the nature of gods]

That you show up only when the need is
Greatest & most dire

Even that's not true
My brain softens & lets you in
That's it, right?

If The Sky Won't Have Me

Or do you push me to
Open the window
You flow through?

Neither

We work together—knowing the other's rhythm
Because, really, we're the same

Transit

Pull down the trees, let in the light
Drain my blood until my
Heart flutters like the butterfly's first wings

We all want to leave that empty place behind,
Escape the cocoon

Drape my finger with a single stone
The color of
Sea glass

So smooth when held

The history of its rough touch,
Wave by wave on
Freezing sand
Carries you forward to a place I will always go

If The Sky Won't Have Me

Twinkling

What is it about you that isn't about me?
Everything
Except where we connect
Overlap
Meld
Trade places
But don't get each other really
Because you're not me after all this time
You're just as much yourself
Grown beyond what I remember
Your voice is the same
Eyes, too, only the lids are more tired
Than they were when you first saw me
From behind
You always say that my face isn't what got
You hooked
I didn't fall in love with your backside/ass/derrière
But it wasn't with your face, either

Anne Leigh Parrish

It was & still is, the twinkling over the
Wild gray lake I sail on as I make for land,
For you, for home

If The Sky Won't Have Me

Anne Leigh Parrish

Still Out There

You're a candle in a glass lantern
& when I light you, you burn,
A dance of energy
Releasing, finding your way to me

Yet we know, deep down,
Love cools when you
Realize you made a bad bet

Affection fades, the heart hungers,
We hollow from the inside out

& so I wonder, gazing at the blackened wick,
If you disappeared because I
Didn't love you enough

But then I see—know—you're
Still out there, burning as brightly as ever,
Perhaps for someone else, or just by
Yourself, alone

If The Sky Won't Have Me

Anne Leigh Parrish

No Matter

Even in the timeless hours, seconds pass
Nothing stops, nothing rests
Dreams open & close like gentle hands
Which in anger turn to fists
Battering flesh & stone
Sometimes there are screams,
A sigh, the occasional sob
Sleep is not death's rehearsal
Just the brain taking a break from
Rational thought
The dreams borne of fear are
Jagged
Those lifted by desire leave one
Hungry
& regret fuels the most fitful sleep—
Whatever the dream,
Or its velvety depth, the first question
On waking is always why,
No matter how I hoped, prayed &
Begged whatever rules your heart,
You didn't love me

If The Sky Won't Have Me

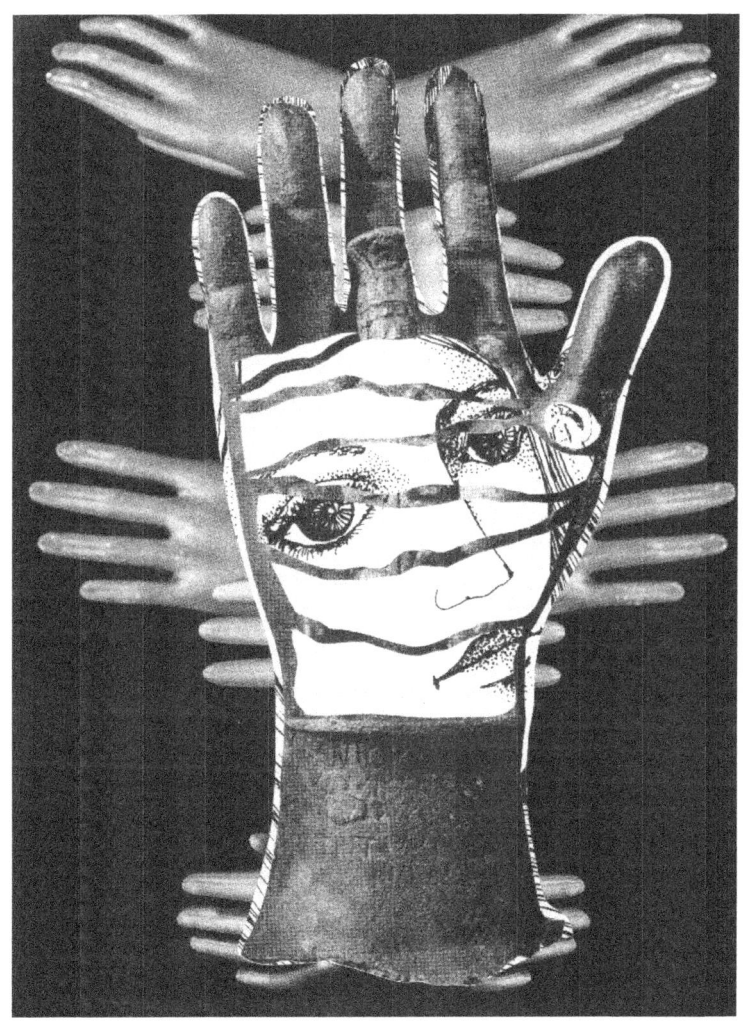

Anne Leigh Parrish

Maybe Love

Maybe love is all that holds us together
Keeping us from breaking away
& forsaking the earth

Maybe faith is the only absolute
Since truth is relative, if you
Think about it enough

Maybe you hear songs in the silence—
A random tap or bang brings back
The notes you loved before

Maybe a heart is stronger than bone
Because it leaps miles in one beat
& destroys you from the inside out

Maybe you've been open so long you don't remember
How to close & be shielded
From the agony of dismissal

If The Sky Won't Have Me

Maybe when the day is done you'll do the
Same again & spend your passion
Until you can barely draw breath

If The Sky Won't Have Me

Wreckage

The world is covered in the wreckage of our sorrow
Here's the lane we drove down as you screamed we were
Through,
The coffee shop we sat outside & wept,
So much brick & glass, asphalt & tar,
Even a fake Japanese pagoda
(The restaurant where I spilled teriyaki sauce on my blouse &
Earned a lecture about my inherent clumsiness)

This, from a man who tripped over his own shoes, left
In the middle of the room

We wade through the grief of tall grass, slip
On the muddy path of rage, plunge
Down the slopes of remorse, land
On a beach we thought was blond, but
Soon turns gray with tears

It's no good, this altering of the world
Maybe we should alter ourselves & tend to what is ours,

Anne Leigh Parrish

The hearts we exchanged, the vows,
The four walls, floor & roof

If we want what we have,
We'll have what we want

I'll be the axis you turn on, you'll be mine,
& round & round we'll go

Until—

One of us veers & crashes into the other &
We litter the world with our broken selves

Gone

A fine view of the sea
From atop
The bluff

A gentle path
Leads through brush,
Open fields, brush again

He dreams of country
Like this, full of surprises &
Shifting light
Lovely to remember but not miss

Wind chops the water
Messes their hair
Chills their hands & feet
Yet they laugh as it
Pushes against them
Almost cruelly
As elements will

Anne Leigh Parrish

They lean into it
A challenge, a test of themselves,
Of their weight & presence
On the earth

Soon it's too hard to walk
Even to stand, she
Falls to the ground
Prays the wind will pass her over
Screams for him to lie
Down too

Her voice is empty

He lifts off, rises, drifts

He's wanted so long
To look down from above
Where everything is small
& she's just another
Feature of the land

If The Sky Won't Have Me

She shelters until
The wind dies
Then gets to her feet

The sky & sea are
Still, calm

What came before
Fades from memory

Until it's gone

Anne Leigh Parrish

Challenge

Before you wade into the ocean
Strip off the glitz & glam
Drop the topaz first
Hear it find the self-embracing shore pine
Next, slide off the diamond
Ignore the twinge
Remember, it's just a fancy piece of carbon
(Aren't you one, too?)

Now your hands are bare
Like his were when he
Closed your eye
& shifted your nose

Rage begets rage
Unless/until it grants absence

The blank space in your chest
Where the heart does its job,
Working above its pay grade,

If The Sky Won't Have Me

Recommends the quiet running down,
The gentle halt to all this insult

But the ocean doesn't want you either
It's too cold, too deep & fast
You dwell on land, so stay there
Stake your claim on the tiniest plot

Challenge yourself to live another day

Anne Leigh Parrish

Resolutions

Tell me of your resolutions
Made as the year winds down
You'll be better, you say
Honest, fair-minded
No more rage, no more
Crushing insults thrown like
Rocks through the window of
My heart

I make resolutions, too,
To tolerate & accept,
Endure & persist,
In essence, to survive

This is how we've hung on for so long
Together we mesh, though one might
Say we're actually co-dependent
Or I enable you

If The Sky Won't Have Me

In matters of love, we choose our
Own storms & then decide
To seek shelter or not

I know you shelter in me
Once, I sheltered in you, though
The time may come when I'm okay
With standing out in the wind
& rain

Keep that in mind, when your
Misery tightens enough to choke us both—
You might become the tree that goes
Down in the forest
With no one there to hear

Anne Leigh Parrish

That Promising Day

I wore my hair down & you slipped on red shoes
The cabinet held the chipped plate
The drawer forgave the bent tines in our
Mismatched forks

Behind the house, in the shade of the big-leaf maple
The river sang to the sapphire jays
Darting to the hazelnut tree

Listen, you said, the river sings for us, too
I strained, but nothing came through

You offered to teach me the tune &
I just couldn't learn

No ear, I said
Your disappointment was quiet, clear

If The Sky Won't Have Me

All this talk of singing poured through me
Opening one door after another
Until the center was met

The notes fell from my mouth like a pearl plucked
From an oyster, or so you said later
When things were hard & we wrapped ourselves
In the memory of that promising day

Anne Leigh Parrish

I Witness My Mother's Death

I stand by as she watches the world leave her
Each day brings a deeper calm
There is no thrashing here
No clutching at the life
Now ebbing

She surveys everything in the room
Me, the bookcase & doorframe with
Acceptance, not fear

It's easy to impute our belief to the dying
& call it truth
When at best it's an observation
Or just hope

Yet there's something there, in those eyes
That glared so sternly when I erred,
Or darkened when I wept

If The Sky Won't Have Me

& naming it, I feel shock
That she would be joyous now
At this final hour

Anne Leigh Parrish

A Lovely Family

How lovely we were in the
Photo, mother & two little girls
I, the younger, held tightly on your
Lap until the camera clicked & you
Pushed me off

It was just for a passport, only a fair
Likeness required yet you wanted to
Arrange your hair
Not for the lens, for the man looking
Through it

How lovely we were in England, then
France, enjoying a picnic lunch with the
Alps behind us & sheep dotting the grass

Your mind was somewhere else,
With someone else,
No one's mother, no one's wife

If The Sky Won't Have Me

How small you seemed from the top of
La Tour Eiffel, a fear of heights kept you
On the ground

You thought you might fall
Or maybe you'd jump

Anne Leigh Parrish

Crossing

No other way to go
Planes too dear
So you set sail
North Atlantic in winter
A fearsome thing

Only sea & sky out there
A study in white & gray
Two days of storms
Toss & roll confining you
To the cabin

Four people, four bunk beds
Private rages, silent hates
Father & mother at odds
Sister despises you
For existing

Ocean calms enough to
Allow a stroll on deck

If The Sky Won't Have Me

Where pitch brings everything
Up, then slowly down
As if water knows how to breathe

At the stern, you stand & watch
A rhythm that has no source
Other than itself, the drop below says
One false step will bring a quick end
To the life you now regret

So you hang on
Tread with care through the
Hours & days
You won't fall, but
Neither will you rise

If The Sky Won't Have Me

Walk On

I'm the blank space you look through
Over & around
Destroy with your ice gaze
Cancel
Negate
Wipe away

Raze the ground under my feet
Sow salt until the
Sweet earth weeps
Blood
Yours & mine
Shared
Thickened by rage, thinned by grief

Time was, I would have
Done anything to
Be seen

Anne Leigh Parrish

Known
Laughed with
Loved

Now I walk on without you gladly

If The Sky Won't Have Me

Her Face Curls

Take from the chest the dress you wore
When she pushed you
Into the river
Down the stairs
Under the bus

Her face curls

Slip into that dreadful rayon
Snagged at the cuffs
From the fight to stay alive

You bested her

It's okay not to be wanted
As long as she keeps her hands
To herself

But she won't

Anne Leigh Parrish

Her face curls

Planning her next attack

Make for the door while her back is turned
Wake sweat-soaked from another nightmare
Remind yourself as your heart now slows

She's gone

Guilt

Oh, how guilt can eat
Such an appetite!
Though it sits in a corner
Its stomach fills the room

The bigger it gets, the less there is
Of you

That's okay
You've been wanting to disappear
Ever since they spent their
Love on someone else

& where is she, this girl
Loaded with kisses & praise?

Waiting for your despair
Love me, love me

Anne Leigh Parrish

She denies you, so you turn your back
Not an easy thing, when you share blood

Hence your fat guilt

But time fills with heartbeats, days & years
& you love so many other people
Guilt thins away
Gives you back the room

If The Sky Won't Have Me

Dollhouse

At the window, I stand & watch the place across the way
My dollhouse, full of decorated dreams about who
Sleeps where
What tiny books sit on tiny shelves
What shoes lie tumbled on the rug

Just ordinary people
But nicer than what I'm used to
Their love flows in shades of orange

Over here, more like a thin brown line

Why can't I be two inches tall with pearl hands & yellow silk
Hair?
A better, prettier self in a house on a table
In a room people walk past & don't touch

My heart's desire = what it's denied

Anne Leigh Parrish

If The Sky Won't Have Me

This Child Of Theirs

The parents crowd in with messy comfort,
So afraid for this child of theirs

When an excited sibling comes too close
& pulls free the tube in his arm
An older boy takes charge

Dashes from the room
Silently seeks help, searches each face
But everyone looks down at screens & clipboards

Except me

When his eyes meet mine they plead for help
I can't give

Then someone who can
Is alerted, tends her miserable patient

I'm forgotten

Anne Leigh Parrish

But only for a time
I'll be found soon enough
Given an update
Spoken to softly
Gently
They'll know more soon
Very soon
Now becomes forever
My child lies dying, too

If The Sky Won't Have Me

These Days

Lost eyes settle on the table that waits
To be cleared
Maybe he's hungry or needs that first
Cup of joe to clear the brain fog
But she knows it won't

Their family knows it too
They beg her to get help
To get him help
She can't talk herself around
He needs her & only her

She tells him it'll just be another minute
The busboy's almost done
But off he goes in a wobbly gait
She worries will bring him down

He makes it, sits,
She does too
I'm hungry, he says

Anne Leigh Parrish

The busboy clears the plates,
The server arrives,
They order, then don't speak
She's used to that

Yet, the easy habit of decades
Isn't quite the same

Once, she was alone with him
Now, she's just alone

He has good appetite,
Yolk rests on his shirt
Soon his mood shifts, as it
Tends to these days

So nice to meet you, he says
& offers her his hand

Green Sun

Our feet are dry,
There's no sign of yesterday's rain

We recognize the high branch bickering,
The shrillness stabbing the ear

But without memory, we don't recall
Despising our soaked shoes, or
The crow's name

The unmoored mind wheels toward safety

Words go, pain stays,
Makes dreadful company

The sun might as well be green

Anne Leigh Parrish

Trick The Prying Eye

To censor is to transubstantiate
Freedom into slavery
War into peace
Orwell said so

Blood is the raven's wing
What's shed, the fallen feather

The birth of symbolism, the rise
Of subtext in centuries of words
Was to trick the prying eye to close
Or at least to look away

Consider fables & fairy tales
Legends & myths in that light

The wolf in the wood is the
Brutal king, the girl with the basket,
His kingdom

If The Sky Won't Have Me

See how firmly we're held
By hidden truth
Story by story

Anne Leigh Parrish

More Softly

Think of the time it takes
For weather to carve a canyon
Peaks to round
Continents to drift
Rivers to dry
Starlight to find us

We've been the people we are now
For only forty thousand years

See what we've done

Ruination & murder everywhere
Species gone forever
Others on the edge of
Blinking out

This is the price of taking
More than we need

If The Sky Won't Have Me

We will always have it,
That urge to destroy & claim

We're not made to sit still
But we can move more softly
When softness is valued & praised

Scientists give us facts
Poets tell us what they mean

Listen to them, not to despots & thugs

Change the conversation, shift the focus

Evolve

Anne Leigh Parrish

Rage

We don't know them before they rage
You think love identifies, or generosity, or
Even the quality of sobs & tears when grief
Holds sway

No

Rage reveals what's concealed by
Manners & convention, what we call social graces

Abandoned for the machine gun &
Confederate flag
Even though the bearers smile
They seethe with hatred
The bitterness of their disenfranchisement
The loss of what . . . exactly?

Free use of the N-word?
Permission to slap their wives & children?

If The Sky Won't Have Me

Once men fought to lift people, not
To oppress them

But times have changed, or perhaps not
Changed at all

Ghosts of slave owners & lynch mobs
Occupy the living

Think about it
Soon you'll feel rage, too

Anne Leigh Parrish

Wake The Hell Up

They hold you in darkness
In order to become the light
Look only to us, they say
We are keepers of the truth

Put away reason
Think magically
Make hope the plan

The world is a mad game of chance
Only the pious win

So pray with us
Hear the gospel

Covid's another flu
It will be gone in a month

Liberate your state
Tear up your masks

If The Sky Won't Have Me

The vaccine will alter your DNA
Give you autism
Or even worse
Make you vote blue

Muon

Don't talk, listen
Until silence coughs &
Dark matter glows

Throw light
Swallow stars
Calculate the transit
Across the heavens
Of a single idea
That contains seventeen
Others
Housed in carbon
Molecules

Accept another end
To a fictitious status quo

Physicists will tell
You everything changes
Even when you're sure

If The Sky Won't Have Me

You know all there is to know
About tides & blossoms
Men & women
How children grow &
Who they become despite your prayers
Wishes, incantations

[Spare them your notion of gender roles
Never works for anyone, anyway
Except for the great white fathers
& they've been lying since the first one opened his mouth]

So, look to the heavens the scientists chart
Not the one said to run by the hand of God

Anne Leigh Parrish

It Never Did

A man, no,
A woman, no,
In this case, it doesn't matter
Just a humanoid
Bipedal, knows how to
Use a tool
Start a fire
Share a language
Not a Neanderthal, it's thought they couldn't
Grasp symbols or sing their children to sleep
Only Homo sapiens did all that
So, anyway, this human, this person with an erect spine
Lives in a cave, litters the floor with bones, old
Tools, pelts, bits of jewelry they get sick of
Or which make them think of someone gone, dead
Then tires of the dark, soot, damp, or dust
Confined like that, only leaving to hunt,
Or haul water, tiresome routines
variety is the spice of life, even then
So, he/she/they venture miles afield,

If The Sky Won't Have Me

Into the light of a burning sun,
To find a screaming mob in pursuit of
A fleeing victim & standing unobserved roots
For the punishment the crowd will give,
Then roots for the victim to escape
& back they/she/he goes into the cave
To wait for people to claim reason over rage
Friendship over hate & madness to pass
But it never did, did it?

Anne Leigh Parrish

A Temple

Better to look like a kid
Skinny & flat chested
Because the minute you become a woman
Men see you as a way to achieve orgasm

Don't call that love

You want to shrink away, so you stop eating

If they can't see you, they can't hurt you
If they can't hurt you, you might have a
Chance
But for what?
To live in a shadow
When they get to stand in the sun

Better to take up residence in yourself,
Be a woman, live like one
Only on your terms, though
No one else's

If The Sky Won't Have Me

Pothole

The pothole broke the axle, then it broke her heart
But that was after the repair guy said, *It's an easy fix*

He talked about his family while he worked
I'm their go-to-guy
I put things back together

She knew the kind, her dad was a fixer, too

All done, the repair guy said,
Now come at me jagged or come at me smooth

She observed the grease on his hands & said, *jagged,*
So he liberated her head
Which, given the circular nature of things,
Landed in the pothole

Lighter, she returned to that grainy depression
In the road

Anne Leigh Parrish

What had distracted her before & pulled her
Eyes away?
Crimson leaves fluttering to earth?
Yellow clouds above the canyon?
A jay so blue his exact color wasn't yet named?

Beauty, always beauty—it got her every time

That man & his dispatching hands,
Even they were beautiful

If The Sky Won't Have Me

Not Seeing Eye To Eye

I call you fake crazy because you're saner than I
You call me crazy fake on account of my lies

You want to be wild, unleashed, out of bounds
I want my words to bring you around

Your distance puts me right at the edge
I've grown too used to gripping that ledge

You tell me to play it straight
I say you'll have a long wait

Never up, always down
Frankly, I'd rather drown

In a sea of ice
Than miss the throwing of rice

You ask, is that what this is about?
I say, please love, have no doubt

Anne Leigh Parrish

In my eye shines a glimmer of truth
Your gray hair says you're getting long in the tooth

You say you never were the marrying kind
& leave me alone to chew on the rind

If The Sky Won't Have Me

Lecture One Of Two

Even in a smudged dappled sky
Light is pointed
Ask Monet, while he makes the heart yearn
Then run wild

Stand back & the scene orders, clarifies, soars
Draw near & proportion slips, softens,
Rearranges into a sonata of color

Like coming close to you
Except your points don't round

Oh, they're bright & sweet, all right
Like the water lilies in Monet's lambent pond

But they dig right through the flesh
To the bone, into the silent spongy
Darkness of my marrow

Anne Leigh Parrish

Lecture Two Of Two

Man: Do you know what a pixel is?

Woman: A unit of clarity

Man: Yes, also no
Think illumination

Woman: There's no light without clarity

Man (short version): It's a computer thing

Man (long version): You're an idiot
God, I wish I knew that about you
Before I wasted my time

So, are we clear?

Woman: As glass

If The Sky Won't Have Me

Threshold

Come in or go out
Are you welcome?
Should you stay or run like hell?
What are these stones at the door?
Do you carry one across, or leave it
When you say good night?
Tribute or trophy?
Everything ends up on average,
In the middle, though not always neutral—
Despite our history,
All the heres & theres,
One side eventually holds sway
Even when we're blind to it—
Just ask the threshold

Anne Leigh Parrish

Our Myths

There is no time in dreams
Everything swims
In the murk of now

Trapped, or held safe?
Whichever—neither or both
It's only for a moment

It all keeps moving

Sea glass is an emerald
The old woman, a girl again
A dog fells the rabbit
I touch your heart

Reason returns when eyes open

& we create our myths
Out of what has left us

If The Sky Won't Have Me

A Gratified Eye

I don't know where things come from, but I know where they
Go
Through the door, down the drain, always away, gone

Yet absence is a temporary state
Memories fill the space where towers of the heart stood,
Blocked the sun, gave luscious, silky shade

Are they real, the moments which return as we walk, kiss,
Bread the chicken, fold socks?

Did we live them, or dream them?

Knowing the difference used to matter,
When everything was named & kept in boxes of our wit

Boundaries lift
Have = had

Anne Leigh Parrish

Now nothing goes, just sits & relaxes in the mind
Until a corner of truth summons
The whole frame for us to view
With a gratified eye

The Seed

I want to be Dorothea Lange
Float in black & white over furrows & fields
Make light in the mind the way she made light on paper
Capture truth
Open hearts
Fire souls

Can the pen deliver as much beauty as the lens?

Do we choose the medium, or does it choose us?

How came Vermeer to paint & not sculpt
Beethoven to write sonatas, not prose?

A seed lies within us that germinates & grows
Why it is one kind & not another
Defies analysis

All that matters is we learn its name

Anne Leigh Parrish

Florist

Thursday's delivery of lilies is substandard, stargazers couldn't
Be had
(New supplier needed)

Friday's hothouse roses are lavish but scent-free,
Like certain personal care products—disappointing!
The weekend is flowerless, which is hard in winter
Too much gray & white everywhere

Monday a crate of African violets you didn't order arrives
(New supplier desperately needed)

They'll probably sell, people love watching
For the first sign of that curled, purple head

Not like an orchid, whose potential
Is usually past tense

What got you into this line of work, anyway?

If The Sky Won't Have Me

A vicarious thrill, maybe
Men in love buying flowers for their ladies
Blushing brides-to-be wanting bouquets

But you don't want to get married, no bridal
Gown for you

Something else drew you here
A need, even hunger

To be surrounded by silence & the complex
Process by which something extraordinary
Simply becomes

Anne Leigh Parrish

For Georgia

She removes the lily stamens so
The table beneath the vase won't
Dust orange-red

Georgia O'Keeffe loved flowers & brought
Us to their center where
Everything gets done

I was there, in her chosen land
All about the light
Hard shadows, sharp rock
Which she captured, too, but
Not as often as things that bloom—
How splendid to have studied them
Hour by hour

I pay for the flowers she hands me, wrapped
Nicely in brown paper & string

If The Sky Won't Have Me

Georgia, I think
These are for you

If The Sky Won't Have Me

On Display

Clothes for sale are on display
Round metal racks hold the excitement of spring
Windows give on the sidewalk
Pedestrians don't look in
If they did, they'd see me
Tricked out in an orange & green dress
My mother thinks will do
I'm going to play Clair de Lune
In a piano recital
Shouldn't my dress invoke moonlight?
Silver & white?
My mother knows best
Which means I keep my mouth shut
The gambit is set
I'll play so gorgeously my garish garb
Will be forgotten
I'll float on & off stage like the music itself
But I'm pigeon-toed & my entrance
Is marred
My exit I don't recall

Anne Leigh Parrish

All that lingered was the piece I played &
The sound of grateful applause

Return

To hear a Chopin nocturne
Is to float in moonlight
To perform it, not so much

Reckoning keys, hard work
But you did it, once

Now the keyboard sits like a row
Of teeth that might bite

You vowed to tame it, long ago
& now, after decades of silence,
It's tamed you

Go back, why don't you
Sit on that hard
Unforgiving bench

Anne Leigh Parrish

When hammer hits string
Find that silver glow
Right where you left it

Almost Perfect

Mozart
Anything in the key of A major
The child's eyes in the woman's face
Caramel apples
Cinnamon on the tongue
Sun on cottonwoods against
A purple sky

The heart lifts, suspended above
Its woe
Beat by beat

The spirit brings forth
Something sublime
& almost perfect

Anne Leigh Parrish

Not All Secrets

Not all secrets are dark
Like moonless nights & basements where the bulb
Went out & got left hanging in the
Socket like a useless arm

Most
I'll give you that

Because carrying them compresses us
Like a black hole
Or the tar patch rolled out on the road

What we don't tell
Becomes secret when we
Yearn to speak

Otherwise, it's just another thing we
Go through & don't share
Like that woman's weird pink shoes
On the bus

If The Sky Won't Have Me

Some secrets are bright-to-blinding,
Solid, sitting in the hand like
A polished stone
Yet light enough to lift & startle us
Into naming joy

If The Sky Won't Have Me

Backstory

The ring is perfectly round
A sphere far better than our home in the heavens
Which is an oblate
Flatter at the poles & wider in between

Absolute perfection is relative
Or non-existent
Or subject to re-evaluation

The finger clad by the ring is
As far from perfect
As cracked plaster is from virgin daub

Flesh is chaos on the grid
The need for mathematical proportion
Always thwarted by asymmetry

The diamond the jeweler prepares to set—
VVS1, E color, round cut, 2 carats—
Was just a stone before,

Anne Leigh Parrish

Nudged from the ground by a callused hand
That will never wear the finished product

We accept the dark backstory because
Despite all we know, the diamond
Throws a rainbow we want to swallow
& become

If The Sky Won't Have Me

Anne Leigh Parrish

Ask The Sea

Everyone is breaking down
A laugh becomes a sob
An eye's cheery glisten brightens to tears

Too long afraid
Too long to be brave

Lie in dark rooms
Scream your voice silent
Cry eyes dry

Lock hope in a blue box
Ask the sea to take it

What good to you now, this ragged
Thing you once were guided by?

If The Sky Won't Have Me

When madness ends &
Fearful men look forward,
Not behind them,
The sea will give it back

Graciously & without having to be asked

Anne Leigh Parrish

Gorgeous Days

The eye remembers what the heart forgets,
The spirit escapes where no light falls

The young man at the door,
There on an errand

The particular this of the particular that,
Wakes the sleeper, lets the griever accept loss

A joyous recall of gorgeous days gone by,
A hunger for those to come

Anne Leigh Parrish

If The Sky Won't Have Me

Come Home

A soft light in the corner draws us in
Blue river on the canvas makes the heart race
What is this place, so quiet, so full?
Talk builds
Talk brings out
Here we have solid dreams in our hands
To spin into the next day & the day after
Blue river meets the edge, finds the sea
We leave our heart's tableau
Light darkens, goes black, hands weaken,
Their grasp lost
Such empty spaces must be filled or
Their emptiness accepted
The blind crave light & the cold
Crave warmth
As to that river on the canvas
Who wouldn't want to call that delicate
Touch her own?
Come home, to the soft light in the corner
& things will flow from there

Anne Leigh Parrish

Lie Down

Lie down, let the earth cover you
Settle among the bones & stone
This is where they want you
Fill with birdsong the hole
In your murdered throat
Let your rotten skin filter rain until streams
Are fed by you
Lie down, join their celebration
Absolve them of their hate
Flow into the sea

If The Sky Won't Have Me

From Joy

Swim to the raft to show you're cool
Not a loser, not a wimp

The cool are always confident

You don't know yet getting somewhere
Comes from work, not conviction

Mad want feels like enough
To make it so

If you tire before the raft, you'll turn back
If not, you'll claim your place

Will you make it?
Just keeping going

If fear rises, logic sinks

Anne Leigh Parrish

You could tell yourself to have faith,
But faith is not fear's opposite
Nor confidence's twin

Faith flows from joy,
The need to celebrate what's beautiful
& beyond our understanding

The raft isn't beautiful & you
Get it just fine

What's beautiful is your body in the water
Gliding forward stroke by stroke

Light, sleek, whole

If The Sky Won't Have Me

See How We Belong

Time softens land & body alike
Though I'd not hasten to compare
My curves to the Appalachians

Water carves canyons, but
Lines on my face don't result
From tears, only laughter

In the heavens, I'd be on my
Way to becoming a white dwarf
Dimmer, yes, but still there

Is it fear of death that makes
Others turn away their gaze?

Even though there are so many like me?

The population is aging, youth
Increasingly rare

Anne Leigh Parrish

Mathematical truths make nothing easier
When you dread your turn to slide
Into waiting ground

Isn't it beautiful, though
To see how we belong
To things that once scared us
& now offer comfort?

Little Cautions

Slow down when the tires slip
Drop the flame when the sauce boils
Pour water for ten seconds, not five
Onto the dry soil of your
Struggling African violet

Endless little cautions
Make a life of prudence

We're not as sturdy as before
More prone to stumble & fall
That's okay
Time wears us hard

No matter if the outside
Shows its age
As long as we're still lit from within

Anne Leigh Parrish

Owner's Manual

When a young woman tends an old one guesses collects
Like rags in a drawer

She must once have been a great beauty, or *How lonely to sit*

By this window day by day

The old one could set her straight if she cared to *Your fella's Not as great as you think he is* & *You should decide now you're not fat*

The human condition starts over with each child born, why
Not issue an owner's manual?

    <u>Part One—Overview</u>
In the wildness of your given years you will:
Despair eight million times, shed rivers of tears
Laugh like a dolphin, weep with joy at the touch of a loved One
Come to rest in a state of quiet amazement

If The Sky Won't Have Me

Like me, she thinks as she's wheeled from the window while
The wheeler vows never to end up like this

Too young to reckon the odds that she probably will

Anne Leigh Parrish

Paths Not Taken

In my body lives a ghost
Not mine, or someone else's
A collection of options
Paths not taken
Choices that blew up or unraveled
When my heart's desire couldn't be found

But I wonder if I'm the sum of my failures
Then surely my moments of glory—
Things I did right & made good on
People I brought into the light—
Exceed them

The ghost keeps score & only she can say
All she does is watch & wait
To see how I'll fare, whether I'll turn left
Or right, stumble, or fall
& how crazily I'll dance

Three Gifts

The first is standing in myself,
Seeing through my eyes, knowing I
Am rooted here alone,
& no one I draw close, adore, fear, or despise
Will ever move me out of it

The second is knowing everyone else,
Every single person, lives in themselves
As completely as I do

The third is theoretical, not yet proven:
My voice touches
Brings joy

If The Sky Won't Have Me

Blue Obsidian

Things of beauty please the eye
Paperweights & polished blocks of lapis & malachite
A small crystal vase with silk roses—pink
My favorite, though I don't care for fake flowers

This place isn't for me

He puts a silver giraffe in my hand
Because I grew tall early
& the teasing I took fell like black rain

Dust motes float in angled light
No rain here

What does he want, this
Curator of his own cluttered greed?

I put the giraffe next to a porcelain girl
In a wide skirt—my skirt & she didn't
Ask to borrow it

Anne Leigh Parrish

So much taking in the world

Yet here's this man, pressing something
Else on me, a smooth stone
He calls blue obsidian

More inspiring than any other color, he says
It can lift & fill the sky
Just like you

If The Sky Won't Have Me

Flatirons

I used to think it was a hard line between level & rise
Daring me, inviting me to cross over
But there is no line
Just one state of things, then another
Gradual yet pointed shift

Took so long to happen
The length of time comforted me
Made me feel my small, fierce self
Was a celebration

& whatever strength or force
Lifted the ground into such a
Fine tilt is still there
Working away
Process by process
All around me

Anne Leigh Parrish

Shift

Backlit clouds suggest a silver shade
Like spilled mercury
Or the cast of a daguerreotype
In the hands of Mathew Brady

Drifting in an unknown sky

Is it loved for its closeness to white
Or because it's nothing like it?

You carry your heart in your shoe
I carry mine in my hand

Yet we both adore the smell of rain

A white-gold band is silver in some light
The promise it stands for shifts, too

Passion becomes patience
Close to love, yet something
Else, entirely

If The Sky Won't Have Me

An Impression

Braided silver shines like
Moon on water
Time tarnishes
Turns gray to gold
Or close enough

Rub it off with a special blue cloth
Use fingernails in a tight space
Work each strand over until
Shine returns

Moon is in her patient glow

Not all stain is gone
Some remains, enough
To give an impression then
Of a gold-&-silver piece

Release of autonomy
Made this marriage

Anne Leigh Parrish

One becoming
The other over time

If The Sky Won't Have Me

Brilliant Country

Lazy skies & slow surf—
I am ready for more
Give me the raging lift of the wave,
The riot of clouds going east
Over the coast range
Where the trees need rest from
Flame & blade

This is my rough, brilliant country
Torn & gorgeous as the sturdy always are

Though I'm slower now with the natural
Tiredness of living, it's delightful to be awed,
Nearly broken by beauty
As I was, the first time here

Anne Leigh Parrish

August

Here you are, with your soft amber lens
Giving this cold discoloration
The hint of a solar eclipse

Somewhere trees are burning
Homes leveled, thousands of acres charred

It's all still far away
Though the news brings it home

No scent of smoke yet but soon

When the lens turns orange
& the long sunset thins away
Into an overdue night

If The Sky Won't Have Me

Put Me Out

If you're rain, I'm drought, dust, fire, sand
Parched earth, searing mountains
A blaze so big you'd see me from space

Put me out, why don't you?

If you're reason, I'm madness, red swirls,
Tattered robes, a raven singing for its supper

The raven has a beautiful voice
Your ear is tin

Maybe you're the china shop & I'm the bull
Yet I help you pick up the pieces

The tiger murders to protect her cubs
Childless, I could kill from rage alone

Stones round after eons of tides

Anne Leigh Parrish

I'm as soft as wind, but we know
What wind can do

The box is too small & the air's all gone
Be what I need, not what I escape from

If The Sky Won't Have Me

In Her Blindness

In her blindness, she quiets,
Pulls from silence
A sigh, blink, heartbeat

In absent light, she gathers
Blackness below the collarbone
A warm inky pool to float in

Color & the stab of sunlight recalled,
Vistas dreamed, faces conjured from love,
Though need no longer rends

Blindness, her best company now,
Sends her along, neither seeking
Nor blessed

Space is black, too
& she's closer to the universe
Than when she could see

Anne Leigh Parrish

The stars—all those passions
Still alive in her bones
Where forever resides

If The Sky Won't Have Me

The rain makes a river of the road
Rushing rivulets, eddies all aswirl

It goes where gravity takes it &
Gathers in a low point, getting deeper
& wider as the storm fails
To relent

I step into the river, reluctantly at first
Then gladly, for I'm ready now to
Be borne away

How easy to drift downstream,
Seeing the familiar yield to the new

The water makes ounces out of pounds
Even hollows bones & maybe I'll lift off soon

Anne Leigh Parrish

If the sky won't have me, the riverbank will
Or the shore, even the ocean depths

It doesn't matter where I come to rest—

I'll stay just until clouds gather,
Rain falls again & I release myself once more

If The Sky Won't Have Me

About the Author

Anne Leigh Parrish is the author of eleven previously published books, most recently *an open door*, a novel, October 2022, and *the moon won't be dared*, poems, October 2021. She lives in the South Sound Region of Washington State, and has joyously ventured into the art of photography. Find at her online at anneleighparrish.com.

About the Artist

Lydia Selk is an artist who resides in the Pacific Northwest with her sweet husband. She has been creating analog collages for several years. Lydia can often be found in her studio with scalpel in hand, cat sleeping on her lap, and a layer of paper confetti at her feet. You can see more of her work on instagram.com/lydiafairymakesart.

About the Press

Unsolicited Press is based out of Portland, Oregon, and focuses on the works of the unsung and underrepresented. As a womxn-owned, all-volunteer small publisher that doesn't worry about profits as much as championing exceptional literature, we have the privilege of partnering with authors skirting the fringes of the lit world. We've worked with emerging and award-winning authors such as Shann Ray, Amy Shimshon-Santo, Brook Bhagat, Kris Amos, and John W. Bateman.

Learn more at unsolicitedpress.com. Find us on Twitter and Instagram: @unsolicitedp.

Printed by BoD in Norderstedt, Germany